PRESSURE MAKES DIAMONDS

Simple Habits for Busy Professionals to Break the Burnout Cycle

VICTORIA HEPBURN

PRESSURE MAKES DIAMONDS

Copyright © 2020 Victoria Hepburn

All rights reserved.
No part of this book may be reproduced, distributed or transmitted
in any form by any means, graphics, electronics, or mechanical, including photocopy,
recording, taping, or by any information storage or retrieval system,
without permission in writing from the publisher, except in the case of reprints
in the context of reviews, quotes, or references.

Paperback ISBN: 978-1-09835-451-0

PRESSURE MAKES DIAMONDS

Simple Habits for Busy Professionals to Break the Burnout Cycle

VICTORIA HEPBURN

DISCLAIMER:

This book is intended for informational purposes only. Users of this guide are advised to do their own due diligence when it comes to making business decisions, and all information, products, and services that have been provided should be independently verified by your own qualified professionals. By reading this guide, you agree that the author is not responsible for the success or failure of your business decisions relating to any information presented in this book.

JUST TO SAY THANK YOU FOR PURCHASING THIS BOOK

I want to give you a special gift – NO COST!

Go to http://victoriahepburn.com/diamond/ for your free Break Your Burnout Habits Checklist ($89 value)

Victoria is available for speaking engagements, book signings, and workshops.
Send your request to booking@victoriahepburn.com

TABLE OF CONTENTS

INTRODUCTION: THE POWER OF RESILIENCE — 1

LETTING GO OF PERFECTION — 6

THE CHALLENGES OF THE AMBITIOUS PROFESSIONAL — 9

THE BOOST FORMULA — 11

ABOUT THE AUTHOR — 19

INTRODUCTION:
THE POWER OF RESILIENCE

I am a business transitions coach who helps and supports professionals who are looking to reclaim their time and joy while they continue to grow and achieve in their careers. Often, I work with busy professionals who are working hard to achieve big goals but have hit a roadblock along the way—for example, overwhelming stress, anxiety, or burnout. If you are one of the many professionals struggling with the effects of workplace stress, you're not alone.

Burnout is reaching epic proportions among professionals in the United States and many other industrialized countries, according to the Association for Psychological Science.[1] The negative effects of burnout spread beyond your professional life and into your physical health and personal well-being. Recent scientific studies[2] have found that burnout is far more than an emotional response to workplace stress; it also affects the health of your brain and body. When you realize that the stress reduction routines and mindsets that made you successful yesterday are not working today, it's frightening. When

---

[1] Michel, Alexandra. "Burnout and the Brain." Association for Psychological Science - APS, 29 Jan. 2016, www.psychologicalscience.org/observer/burnout-and-the-brain?fbclid=IwAR3dLcprutFthmXIZkglhE2qxNa5li-Va_RZAD-6qzJBIJ7VTr2zhDs9Aoa8.

[2] Salvagioni, D., Melanda, F. N., Mesas, A. E., González, A. D., Gabani, F. L., & Andrade, S. M. (2017). "Physical, psychological and occupational consequences of job burnout: A systematic review of prospective studies." PloS one, 12(10), e0185781. https://doi.org/10.1371/journal.pone.0185781; Reith T. P. (2018). Burnout in United States Healthcare Professionals: A Narrative Review. Cureus, 10(12), e3681. https://doi.org/10.7759/cureus.3681.

under this type of stress, you're pushing forward and going nowhere. One of my coaching clients described it as if you are trying to run underwater. Still, you continue to push forward because you're committed to getting results and don't want to let your team down even though you know you are wearing yourself out. This cycle of feeling overwhelmed and getting stuck is how people start to feel professional exhaustion, or burnout.

Wanting to stop this tense situation brings many of my clients to start a custom coaching program with me. I designed the BOOST coaching program based on my process that has helped busy professionals successfully build up their stress resilience, grit, and passion. Once they reclaim their values and power, new possibilities emerge in their lives. The program helps people shift their perspective on their challenges and unlock their inner strength to quickly recover from setbacks and calmly resolve tough situations. Studies have repeatedly shown people who have more grit and resilience are more likely to achieve their goals and bounce back from crises faster. They also have a better overall quality of life, including better health, more joy, more motivation, and more control of their lives.[3]

My coaching program is designed to help you get unstuck, move forward in your goals, and build up your resilience to stress. It's a space to name and tame whatever is blocking you from feeling joy and hitting your goals. The program gives you support and accountability to adopt the mindset you need to confidently reach your goals. We work together as client and coach to create solutions that are custom-tailored to build up your resilience to setbacks so you can confidently leap toward your goals and live a life you love.

My target audience consists of professionals frustrated with their career journey and ready to make changes to significantly increase their clarity, impact, and happiness. My clients are hardworking, values-driven women and men who have demanding and often hectic work situations. One client

---

[3] Jachimowicz, J. M., Wihler, A., Bailey, E. R., & Galinsky, A. D. (2018). Why grit requires perseverance and passion to positively predict performance. Proceedings of the National Academy of Sciences of the United States of America, 115(40), 9980–9985. doi:10.1073/pnas.1803561115.

described that his daily work issues come at him as fast as if he's trying to "drink out of a fire hose." My clients have big ideas and big responsibilities. Juggling all of those responsibilities—at work, at home, and in the community—can be overwhelming at times, but they don't want to quit. Unlocking the power of resilience accelerates your ability to navigate your full and busy life with clarity, confidence, and joy.

Stress is the natural byproduct of pushing through challenges to achieve your goals. While you can't avoid stress, you can get better at responding to stress and bouncing back from it quickly. Resilience is your ability to "bounce back" from setbacks quickly and without losing your sense of direction or energy. Resilience isn't some magic spell that will remove obstacles or pain; it lessens the time you wallow in frustration or anxiety and keeps you aligned with your passions, purpose, and goals.

This book is called *Pressure Makes Diamonds* because I want professionals to know that their pain has a purpose. Diamonds are precious gems formed deep within the earth under intense heat and pressure. When they are pulled from the earth, they can look like unremarkable sparkly rocks. Diamonds get more beautiful when many facets are cut into them, allowing their brilliance to show. In this way, people are similar to diamonds. Often, the most successful people have gone through intense pressures and have many facets—talents, wisdom, character, personality—that make them seem irresistible to others.

I started learning about resilience years ago because I was desperate to break my own workplace stress burnout cycle. Before becoming an author and business transitions coach, for many years, I worked in corporate engineering and sales roles at large international firms. In those corporate roles, I learned firsthand how busy and stressful life can get. I worked long hours to solve customer issues with millions of dollars on the line, which stressed my body, mind, and spirit many times. In one role, I was working on projects in five time zones because my US clients had partners in Europe and Japan, and my team was spread out in North America, Europe, and Asia. Complicated doesn't begin to describe it.

When I first started experiencing exhaustion, weight gain, cynicism, brain fog, back pain, indigestion, and poor sleep, my friends pointed out that those were my wake-up calls that I needed to make major changes in my life. Luckily for me, I have a great network of friends who are also in high-stress, high-reward careers and share their struggles and solutions with me. It's a gift to have people around you who also know that "work-life balance" is a myth and "work-life juggling" is more practical.

Initially, I thought burnout was something I had to put up with since everybody around me was going through crazy stressful days and getting run down as well. Plus, it felt like too big of a problem for me to solve. I tried, but I had no idea what to do. So I started researching like my life depended on it and figured out a way to break my burnout cycle. I invested time and money because I wanted real-life, sustainable transformation. The transformation I got after spending time learning and practicing new tools and after spending thousands of dollars training with business and mindfulness experts was nothing short of a miracle. Before I share that with you, let's talk about why I'm taking the time to write this book.

I want busy professionals everywhere to have the tools and support to stop feeling frustrated, anxious, and stressed all the time so they can confidently achieve their career goals. It's my mission to help the people who are working to make the world better, who want to grow their communities, and who are passionate about creating amazing results, not just for their businesses but also for their communities and families. These people make the world a better place and create a brighter future for our planet through their hard work and innovation.

After reading this book, the number one lesson I want you to take away is that you can get back on the path to loving your life without stopping your career or settling for less than you deserve. I know it may be difficult for some readers to believe, but you can resolve old challenges that block your professional progress without waiting for someone else to change. This is true for me, my clients, and many other busy professionals—and it is true for you.

When it is obvious that the goals cannot be reached, don't adjust the goals, adjust the action steps. —Confucius

LETTING GO OF PERFECTION

As a coach, I get to work with highly motivated professionals who consistently produce results in complicated situations. When we start working together, they often share that they are feeling frustrated, lost, or miserable with how things are going but know that they can do better for themselves. In the process of coaching, I support clients by asking questions and sharing scientifically proven strategies to build confidence and resilience. When needed, I challenge them with healthy doses of tough love and hold my clients accountable for the goals they set.

After hundreds of hours of coaching busy professionals, I noticed that one of the most common stressors is the quest for perfection. Often they are stressed out and frustrated because they cannot get themselves or other people to conform to their highest expectations. They say things like:

- "I'm amazed I get anything done in a day with everyone making demands of my time."
- "I need to do more to prove myself."
- "I'm constantly putting out fires and never seem to get to the work I need to do."
- "I need more hours in the day."
- "If you want something done right, you might as well do it yourself."

The thing that fuels my passion for coaching is witnessing the transformations that people achieve when they commit to looking at their lives differently. After clients start using my proven techniques, the dialogue with my clients starts to transform:

- "Oh my goodness, after we spoke last week, this amazing thing happened."
- "I got clarity on something I've been struggling with for years."
- "I couldn't figure out how to respond to this mess before, and now I have picked my path, I'm so confident, and my business is taking off."

My clients get these results quickly because they are open to letting go of perfection. They let go of the idea that someday some external force will change your life for the better. They stop waiting for others to do what they think they "should" do.

In order to move forward beyond my burnout cycle, I had to release perfection too. I very much wanted things to be a certain way, and I wanted to be the best version of everything, which is part of why I worked so many long hours. You cannot build forward momentum toward your goals if you are looking for perfection. A wise person once told me, "Perfection is the enemy of progress." Some successful artists, like Monet, have said they didn't love their most acclaimed works because that wasn't the best version they think they could've produced. Think about all the joy and inspiration we would have missed out on if Monet had held his work back or destroyed it for not being perfect. Even though they felt they could've done better, they didn't let that notion of perfection stop them from taking action to put their work out there.

For me, even bigger than the need for perfection was the need to please people. I wanted people to like me, to see me as a team player, and to see me as competent and helpful. If you are a people pleaser, you bend over backward to do things for people who probably would never do the same for you; and those people probably don't appreciate the sacrifices that you're making for them. To overcome this need to be liked, it took some coaching to shift my mindset to align with my goals. I had to get clear on where my energy needed to be and what I was willing to let go.

If there is no struggle, there is no progress. —Frederick Douglass

THE CHALLENGES OF THE AMBITIOUS PROFESSIONAL

My clients come to me to learn tools to help reframe their business challenges and uncover their ability to navigate their career journey with less stress and anxiety. The question they ask frequently is, "What can I do to build up my confidence quickly?" They are busy professionals in career transitions and business expansions who want to reclaim time to work on purpose-driven projects and recover from an overachieving, workaholic lifestyle. My clients are intelligent and hardworking people who know how to focus on their future goals while overcoming past challenges. They are looking for a shortcut to get back to loving their lives while still thriving in business.

Another specific challenge my clients are facing is the "always-on" work culture. Along with managing very demanding businesses and customers, my clients struggle to meet the high expectations they have set for themselves. They feel frustrated and don't know exactly how to get their lives on the right track. Throughout the day, there are daily crises that erupt that they have to jump into and quickly resolve. These distractions train the brain to look for more emergencies and block people from being able to step back to strategically review their work or career options. They work on their phones at home after hours and on vacation, so their minds never really get a break. Often, there's not enough time for rest, so they become sleep deprived. Many also tend to have poor diets that zap their energy.

On top of all these busy professionals have to deal with, there's often an ever-present fear that drives them. Fear of failure, fear of letting others down, fear of being found out as an imposter, fear of success, and fear of missing out on opportunities, to name a few. I work with many clients on overcoming imposter syndrome: they know they have achieved so much, yet they don't necessarily feel qualified to be in their role, leading to the self-imposed pressure to "prove themselves."

One of the big ideas that helps my clients transform their relationship with stress is shifting perspective from reactive to proactive. You can't change other people, but you can always change your attitude and response to them. What would change for you if you stopped waiting for other people to "act right" or "do things the right way"? My clients are relieved to learn that they can get quick results when they commit to trying new habits. With my help, they get to experience the amazing power of small changes, support, and accountability.

We may encounter many defeats, but we must not be defeated.
—Maya Angelou

THE BOOST FORMULA

I find that most people know what they want, yet few are clear on how to get it. It's easier to follow a process than spend time trying and failing until you get the desired outcome. I developed the BOOST formula to give busy professionals a proven blueprint to stop feeling frustrated and remove their personal roadblocks on their path to success.

There's a process that I go through with many of my private coaching clients. Since you're reading this e-book, I'll share it with you too. First, you must commit to getting your life off autopilot and trying a new routine for at least a month. You will need to take new actions and set new intentions to create lasting change in your life. The BOOST formula is based on a lot of research on positive psychology, the science of happiness, and business productivity.

BOOST is the acronym that stands for:

Be specific.

Organize your priorities.

Operate as a leader.

Share responsibility with others.

Take time for yourself.

Be specific.

You have to be intentional in your work, especially if you are in an environment that has a lot of crises and things you have to jump on right away. All those micro-stresses can put your brain in a state of psychological hyper-vigilance, where you're constantly reacting to events, but you lose your ability to prioritize your workload. In these conditions, your brain gets impaired and develops a bias toward negative emotions and thoughts, especially when you're dealing with high-level tasks. You lose your ability to quickly calm yourself, be creative, or stay focused. Your brain cannot function without adequate self-care. The elements of self-care are necessities and not luxuries; sleep, hydration, nutrition, positive social connections, appreciation, and regular breaks from thinking are required. I recommend tracking these self-care elements in a journal, spreadsheet, or app. There is a free daily accountability spreadsheet included in the free gift at victoriahepburn.com/diamond.

At work, be conscious of your time and set clear start and end points for your workday, meetings, and project work. What are the measurable outcomes for the big things that you're working on? Often, your day can be thrown off by a simple request like someone saying, "Hey, give me a report on the latest sales revenue versus forecast." Remember that it's okay to ask a clarifying question to save you some time. "Well, do you want quarter to date, year to date, month to date?" or "All the sales force or just in the United States?" Be very specific to ensure you expend the minimum amount of your time to deliver the maximum value to your stakeholders.

Organize your priorities.

Most people address what screams the loudest in their inbox, which often is not necessarily the most important thing they need to be doing in that moment or day. In order to control your schedule, you need to identify and organize your priorities. One way to get organized at the end of your workday is to make a short list of the critical tasks that you need to accomplish for the next day. Then, at the start of your next workday, set aside time early in the day to complete those critical tasks by turning off your distractions. Turn off your phone alerts, turn off your email alerts, and turn off any other alerts that you might have; in that allotted time, work on addressing those few important tasks. That way, when emergencies pop up, you'll be able to give them your full attention because you already completed the day's critical tasks.

Operate as a leader.

Leaders have to make tough choices every day. They have to focus on the big picture and take decisive action. Often, professionals get stressed out from weighing options and "what if" scenarios in our minds. At times like this, it's important to have trusted advisors and mentors to hear your idea out loud and offer supportive feedback. These advisors and mentors could be people on your team, people in your business network, or your trusted friends. It should be someone you trust who understands your position and responsibility and will make time for you. This process allows you to hear your thoughts out loud instead of continuing to flip them over constantly in your mind, which drains your energy and steals time.

Leaders must be present to make clear decisions. If you are worrying about things in the past or projected into the future, you aren't focusing on the present moment. You lose time that you can never get back, and your worry can negatively affect people in your life. None of us are as great at hiding our emotions as we think we are. In order to build clarity and focus, you must practice being in the present moment. Meditation, yoga, and mindfulness practices are great tools that help you practice shifting your attention to the present moment.

Next time your thoughts trigger anxiety, embarrassment, or anger that distracts you, try a proven strategy to redirect it. I learned this strategy from famous brain researcher Dr. Daniel Amen and later expanded on it through studying Byron Katie's self-reflection process. The process is simple. Hold that negative thought and allow yourself to feel it, pause, and ask yourself these questions:

- "Is that really true?"
- "What happens to me when I believe that thought?"
- "If I stop believing that thought, who would I be?"

If you take a few moments to do this process, it has the amazing ability to shift your energy and attention back to the people and work ahead of you.

Share responsibility.

The secret here is that you don't have to know everything and you don't have to do every task to be successful in life or business. You do need to know the right people who you can trust to help you and work with you to achieve the same goal. If you have a great team, great outcomes are possible. Sometimes you walk into a position and there's a team already in place. Sometimes, as an entrepreneur, you have to pull together the right team in order to grow and scale quickly. Always keep in mind that your team is your magical secret to lowering your stress levels. When you share your vision and values, other people can invest in your goals and outcomes. They will want to contribute to the team's success. People will surprise you with tremendous contributions when they feel trusted, capable, and committed.

In order to get people enrolled in your outcomes, whether you're their manager or peer, or maybe you're influencing a more senior leader, you have to build rapport. Be intentional and get on their calendar for work meetings and some social time, like a lunch or coffee break. Say hello when you see them in the office; acknowledge their efforts to pull together a report or efforts to keep supporting the customer during a crisis; do the little things you can to build a positive working relationship over time. Be sincere and real. If you're a manager, consider putting "office hours" on your calendar each week and holding a meeting or video conference where your direct reports (and maybe other team members you often work with) can drop in and share what they are working on or grateful for with each other. You can start off by reflecting on a personal or professional win that a team member is celebrating. Before sharing a team member's news, be sure to ask permission ahead of the meeting via email, chat, or text to make sure they know they will be in the spotlight in advance.

If you're remote, make time for coffee chats (up to ten minutes of small talk) and set up regular check-in meetings with key team members. Be sure to get to know them as a full person beyond their work persona. Be friendly and don't pry as you check-in on their life updates—ask them how they are doing, how their families are doing, what their weekend plans are, or how their vacation was—before you go into work talk. Get excited about things that you have in common, like music, kids, or a mutual love-hate relationship with your favorite TV show. Whatever it is, the goal is to find some commonality, get them to see you as a person, and to show that you see them as a person beyond work. In my corporate sales career, these behaviors helped me get my projects expedited because my internal teammates were more connected to me than some of my colleagues who didn't make an effort to know them. It doesn't take a lot of effort in order to make those connections, and it makes work more fun and meaningful.

Take time for yourself.

Again, an important element of this step is creating a support system—friends, family, close colleagues—that you can reach out to when you need a break or when you're in crisis mode. I have a great friend who, if I say, "Hey, let's plan a trip, let's go somewhere," she's like, "Okay, when? I have some ideas." We share that wanderlust and need to explore. Our trips also give us something to look forward to beyond the day-to-day work struggles.

Another way I take time for myself is by spending time with my high-energy rescue dog, who loves being outside. I don't recommend this unless you're willing to commit to taking care of another precious being, but it really helped me step outside my house every single day, twice a day, and interact with my neighbors. I got more exercise, and I ultimately learned how lovely my neighborhood is. I start my days refreshed from our morning walk and get a nice decompression from the workday during our evening walk. I am so thankful to have this amazing dog in our family.

All work and no play doesn't just make you dull; it makes you lonely, anxious, depressed, and exhausted. You have to design your schedule so you can get up and move your body for a few minutes many times throughout the day. Research shows that your focus on high-level tasks improves when you take time away from work and get out of your head for a bit. It's reported that Albert Einstein used to ride his bicycle or play his violin when he was on a break from a tough physics problem. If it worked for one of the twentieth century's greatest thinkers, it's worth a try.

Another powerful way to rewire your brain is to consistently schedule time with people you look forward to seeing. As a busy professional, it's so easy to cancel plans with family and friends, even on weekends, because you need to get this project done or that client proposal out. I lived that way and want you to understand it's a miserable trap. Keeping healthy relationships with the people who matter to you is critical to your overall success. So reach out and put time to get together on your calendars. Book a concert for a band you both like or another event that you would feel very, very sad to cancel, if that has been your history. If you want to start with smaller steps, maybe invite some friends over for game night or meet up at your favorite restaurant for dinner—whatever is in your comfort zone. For one of my clients, this meant planning a vacation with an old friend because she could have fun and be her true self. Whatever it is, make sure you take the time to take a bold action that supports your well-being.

If you don't have that big of a friend circle and you're looking to expand it, go to more events—in person and virtual. There are lots of events you can attend to meet people: on social media, volunteer events, professional networking events, hackathons, and meet-ups for all types of interests.

I've used Meetup.com and met some amazing people. I also made wonderful friends when I volunteered at the World Science Festival and when I joined the Sustainable Jersey Green Team in my city.

People are unique, and our energy sparks brightest through connection. Find people you like, who inspire you, who think in ways you find interesting. That will help you remember who you truly are away from your work and build up resilience. A key to building resilience is knowing you are not alone, knowing that you have support in this world. Whether this support comes from your family from birth or the family you choose, having that structure and that stability makes your journey easier and more fun.

The power of these practices enabled me to have a better quality of life than I had imagined, and the only thing that changed was my perspective. I didn't have to stop my career journey or leave a job I enjoyed. I was able to spend more time with the people I care about because I wasn't preoccupied with work or worrying about other things I did but wish I had done differently. Having lower stress levels helped me remember what's important to me and where I should spend my time and energy. As much as I enjoyed my work, I realized that I needed to create more space for self-care, fun, community, and relationships.

Next Steps

I'm here to serve you if . . .

- You are a corporate professional ready to use proven tools to reclaim your time and energy so you can earn more and live well.
- You want support from an expert coach with a proven system to build up your confidence and clarity to reach your goals faster.
- You are ready to embrace new habits and perspectives to create great business results and get back on the path to loving life.

LET'S CONNECT!

Email: info@victoriahepburn.com

Twitter: @V_HepburnAuthor (mention #HepburnWisdom)

ABOUT THE AUTHOR

Victoria Hepburn, ACC, is quickly becoming a leading expert on employee well-being and transformational leadership. As an author, a motivational speaker, and an internationally certified business coach, she partners with individuals and organizations seeking to use proven tools to strengthen their confidence, focus, and drive as they grow in their careers and businesses.

Ms. Hepburn earned a Bachelor of Science in Chemistry from New York University and a Bachelor of Chemical Engineering from Stevens Institute of Technology through a dual degree program. She earned several top sales awards while working at Fortune 500 companies like GE Healthcare and BD. She is an IPEC certified professional coach, is a certified Heartmath Coach/Mentor, and was awarded an Associate Certified Coach (ACC) accreditation by the International Coaching Federation. She lives in New Jersey with her family and cuddly rescue dog who refuses to play fetch.

Victoria is available for speaking engagements, book signings, and workshops. She speaks to audiences – both live and virtually – about how ambitious professionals can navigate the chaos and overwhelm on their success journey. Energetic and frank, she shares road-tested strategies and simple tips, inspiring serious business leaders to accelerate their growth through the power of resilience and work/life integration.

To engage Victoria as a speaker or coach or to make individual or quantity purchases of her book, "Pressure Makes Diamonds", get in touch today.

Email: booking@victoriahepburn.com

Website: www.VictoriaHepburn.com